BANNOCKBURN SCHOOL DIST. 106
2165 TELEGRAPH ROAD
DEERFIELD, ILLINOIS 60015

Corn
Chowder

Poems by
James Stevenson
with illustrations by the author

Greenwillow Books
An Imprint of HarperCollins*Publishers*

Watercolor paints and a black
pen were used to prepare
the full-color art.

Library of Congress
Cataloging-in-Publication Data

Stevenson, James, (date).
Corn chowder /
by James Stevenson.
    p.   cm.
"Greenwillow Books."
Summary: A collection of
short poems with titles such
as "At the National Zoo,"
"Cell Phone," and
"Backpack Mystery."
ISBN 0-06-053059-6 (trade).
ISBN 0-06-053060-X (lib. bdg.)
1. Children's poetry, American.
[1. American poetry.]   I. Title.
PS3569.T4557 C64 2003
811'.54—dc21   2002009111

1 2 3 4 5 6 7 8 9 10
First Edition

For Leo, with love

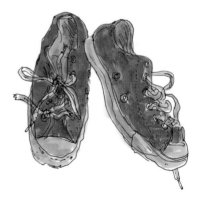

Contents

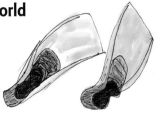

In
the
city,
dogs
are
put
in
charge
of . . .

trees,

signs,

and parking meters.

At Harry's Fresh Flowers,

everything is bright and cheerful.

Except Harry.

Plenty of pencil left, but the eraser's gone.
Somebody must keep changing his mind.

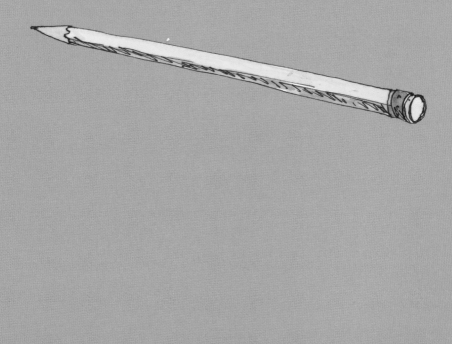

The baby elephant runs.

It stands in a tub and a tire.

It walks under
its mother.

The baby giraffe
stretches its legs,

while
the panda
sits quietly
in a tree.

When you think
everything is
falling apart,
look how many ways
there are
to hold things
together.

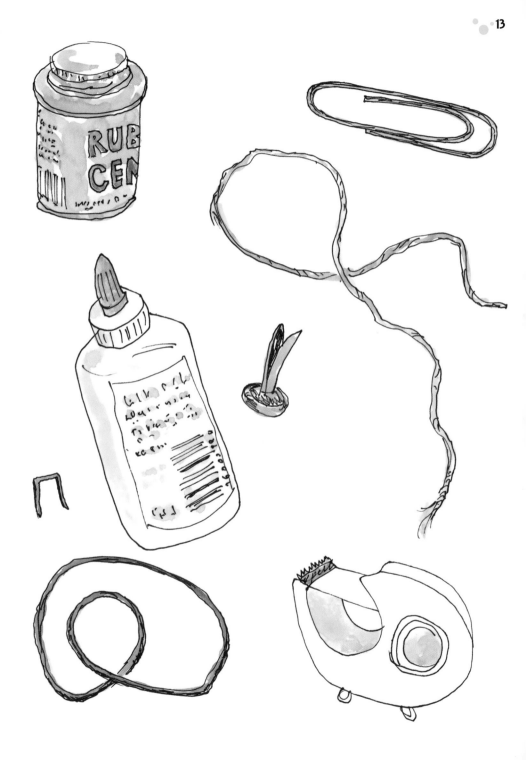

Some climb up.

Some slide down.

Some fly in the air.

Some sit . . .

and watch.

Some whirl around.

Some **bounce.**

Some sleep in the shade.

Some eat **S N A C K S** .

Some take one more slide.

And some go home.

TO PEOPLE I HEAR TALKING LOUDLY ON THEIR CELL PHONES

It is **VERY IMPORTANT** to take care of your cell phone! Do you know how?

The best way is to drop it in a deep pot of chicken fat and bring to a boil.

Simmer for two hours.

Let cool.

OW! OW! OW!

It feels like somebody shot an arrow

through my forehead . . .

OW!

But wait . . . The pain is

slowly going away . . . Ahhhh . . .

It's gone, and now it's safe

(I hope) to take another bite

of that icy-cold,

delicious

ice cream.

Did you ever have an idea come along,

a pretty good idea,

and the more you thought about it,

the better it got

and the fancier it got

until it was
a really great idea,

one of
the best ideas
you ever had,

but then somebody else said, **"What a dumb idea!"**

and it all fell down . . .

and you had to wait for the next idea?

I WISH I HAD LIVED ONE HUNDRED YEARS AGO IN MEXICO.
I WOULD HAVE BEEN A **VAQUERO**, ROUNDING UP CATTLE,

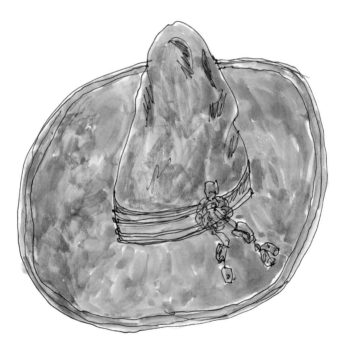

WEARING A HAT LIKE THIS.

Or I would have been a cowboy in Texas,
with a saddle like this . . .

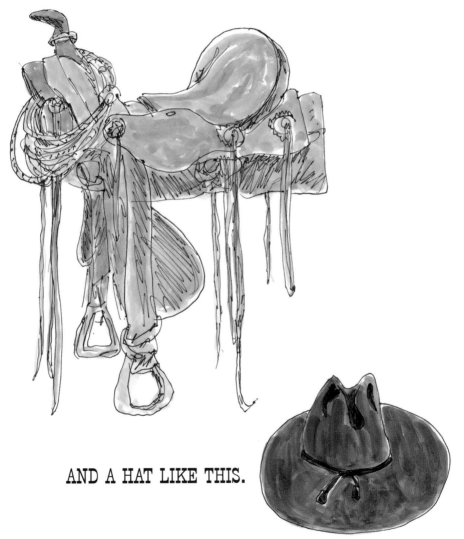

AND A HAT LIKE THIS.

When I go to the drugstore and

I am grateful to be

see how many ailments there are,

ALIVE.

Everybody's
waiting
for something
in the city:

for the talk to end,

for a taxi,

for the bus to arrive,

for the time to pass,

for the light to change,

for the truck to come.

The
children
go to
school
with
backpacks
so big,
it makes
you
wonder
what's
inside
them.

A BOWLING BALL ?

A CINDER BLOCK ?

A BOX OF
JELLY DOUGHNUTS ?

AN ACCORDION ?

A PUMPKIN ?

THE FAMILY DOG ?

A BOWL OF
GOLDFISH ?

BREAD, BOLOGNA, MUSTARD?   CHEESE, LETTUCE, MAYO?

200 TRADING CARDS?

A DOZEN OVERDUE LIBRARY BOOKS?

TWO SKATEBOARDS?

A RAINCOAT, A TENT, AND A SLEEPING BAG?

MORE HAIR RIBBONS. AND AN ELECTRIC IRON?

A WEEK'S SUPPLY OF JELLY BEANS?

EVERYTHING YOU COULD NEED IN THE COURSE OF THE YEAR?

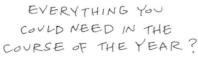

SOME KIDS HAVE BACKPACKS SO HEAVY, THEY HAVE TO BE WHEELED TO SCHOOL.

An American Goldfinch
is at work on his "Field Guide to Human Beings."

A can of paint

always

has more in it

than you need,

and it

lives with you

for the rest of your life.

The museum is a good place

for the very young . . .

and the very old . . .

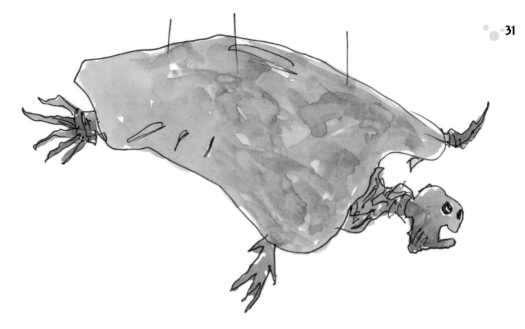

and the *very* brave.

Do you ever wonder how much peanut butter you have had in your life?

I have had
T H I S *much,*
and I am about to buy another jar.

Under the bridge where the highway crosses the river,

somebody has put a folding chair.

Maybe the person just likes to eat his lunch

and listen to the thunder of the traffic overhead.

Q: *What do you get when you take small children to breakfast at the diner?*

IF you look
in the locksmith's window,
you'll see there is more
than one way to open a door.

Trees on the sidewalks grow

in boxes of dirt,

in bricks,

behind bars,

inside wire fences,

in gravel.

The trees don't always make it,

but a lot of the time they do.

On a sweltering night in July in the city,
the snack wagon rolled out of its garage.
It rattled down the empty streets
and into Central Park.

When a breeze came up,

the snack wagon went for a sail on the lake.

Then it rolled back home to the garage,

leaving only a trail of drips.

Q: Are these flying objects in outer space?

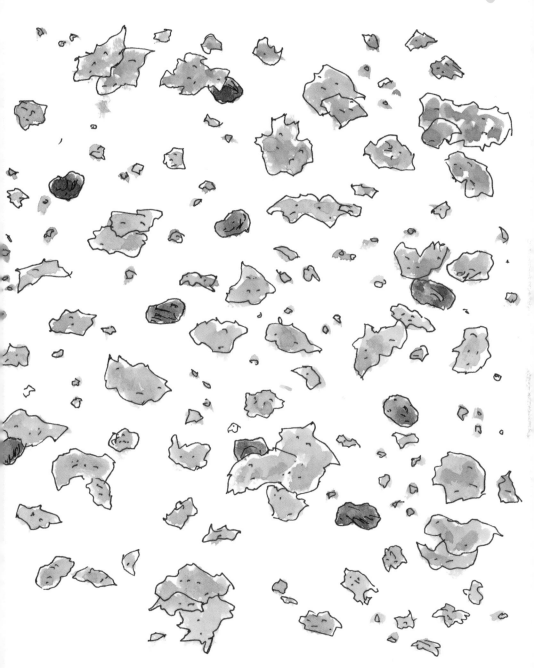

A: No. This is what happened when I dropped the box of Raisin Bran on the kitchen floor.

Sometimes I wish the turnpike was

the way it used to be.

There's
a noise
so loud,

there is
nothing
louder . . .

than Uncle Carl eating
his sweet corn chowder.

BANNOCKBURN SCHOOL DIST. 106
2165 TELEGRAPH ROAD
DEERFIELD, ILLINOIS 60015